Sports Records

Olympic Records

by Karen Price

FOCUS READERS

BEACON

www.focusreaders.com

Focus Readers is distributed by North Star Editions:
sales@northstareditions.com | 888-417-0195

Produced for Focus Readers by Red Line Editorial.

Photographs ©: Kin Cheung/AP Images, cover, 1; Thomas Kienzle/AP Images, 4; David J. Phillip/AP Images, 7; Petr David Josek/AP Images, 8; Markus Schreiber/AP Images, 11; Kazuki Wakasugi/Yomiuri Shimbun/AP Images, 13; David Goldman/AP Images, 14–15; AP Images, 16, 29; Daniel Karmann/picture-alliance/dpa/AP Images, 19; Bela Szandelszky/AP Images, 21; Eric Gay/AP Images, 22; Victor R. Caivano/AP Images, 24; Julie Jacobson/AP Images, 26

Library of Congress Cataloging-in-Publication Data
Names: Price, Karen (Sports writer), author.
Title: Olympic records / by Karen Price.
Description: Lake Elmo, MN: Focus Readers, 2021. | Series: Sports records | Includes index. | Audience: Grades 4-6
Identifiers: LCCN 2020012321 (print) | LCCN 2020012322 (ebook) | ISBN 9781644933633 (Hardcover) | ISBN 9781644934395 (Paperback) | ISBN 9781644935910 (PDF) | ISBN 9781644935156 (eBook)
Subjects: LCSH: Sports records--Juvenile literature. | Olympics--Juvenile literature. | Winter Olympics--Juvenile literature. | Athletes--Rating of. | Olympic athletes.
Classification: LCC GV741 .P75 2021 (print) | LCC GV741 (ebook) | DDC 796.02/1--dc23
LC record available at https://lccn.loc.gov/2020012321
LC ebook record available at https://lccn.loc.gov/2020012322

Printed in the United States of America
Mankato, MN
082020

About the Author

Karen Price is a longtime newspaper reporter turned freelance writer who has been covering sports for more than 20 years. She lives in Pittsburgh, Pennsylvania, with her husband and their four cats.

Table of Contents

speedo

Chapter 1

Fantastic Phelps

American swimmer Michael Phelps stepped onto the starting block. He was ready for his first race at the 2008 Olympics. The record for most gold medals at one Olympics was seven. Phelps wanted eight.

Michael Phelps competes in the 400-meter individual medley at the 2008 Olympics.

Phelps was swimming in the 400-meter **individual medley**. He hadn't lost that race in six years. Halfway through the race, Phelps had a small lead. On the last two laps, he pulled ahead. Phelps won the race. He also smashed the world record.

Phelps set a total of seven world records at the 2008 Olympics. And he won eight gold medals. That was the most ever at one Olympic Games.

In addition to his 23 gold medals, Phelps won silver three times and bronze twice.

Phelps didn't stop there. He competed in five different Olympic Games during his career. In total, Phelps won 23 gold medals. That's more than any athlete in any sport.

XXX Olympiad London

Chapter 2

Summer Records

American volleyball players Misty May-Treanor and Kerri Walsh Jennings were nearly unstoppable. Most experts say they were the best beach volleyball team ever.

Misty May-Treanor (left) and Kerri Walsh Jennings celebrate their victory at the 2012 Olympic Games.

The duo competed in three Olympic Games. And they won three gold medals in a row. No other beach volleyball team has ever done that.

Wrestling Powerhouse

Kaori Icho is a **wrestler** from Japan. For 13 years, she didn't lose a single match. She went to every

Fun Fact

At the first modern Olympics in 1896, winners didn't receive gold medals. They received silver coins and wreaths of olive leaves.

Kaori Icho's 13-year winning streak totaled to 189 matches.

Summer Olympics from 2004 to 2016. And she won gold every time. Icho set a record as the only woman to win an individual gold medal at four back-to-back Olympics.

Arrow Aimed for Gold

Kim Woojin is an **archer** from South Korea. At the 2016 Olympics, he scored 700 out of 720 points. He shot his last six arrows. Four arrows landed in the middle of the target. The fifth arrow dropped outside.

Fun Fact

Olympic gold medals are not made of pure gold. They are covered in gold on the outside. But they have a less expensive metal on the inside.

Kim Woojin set records during qualifications for the 2020 Olympic Games.

But his last arrow struck the middle. His score set a new Olympic and world record.

IMPOSSIBLE TO BREAK?

Horsing Around

Ian Millar was 10 years old when he first rode a horse. Millar became a talented **equestrian**. He competed in show jumping for Canada. When Millar was 25, he competed in his first Olympics. But it was far from his last. He has been to more Olympics than any other athlete. In all, Millar took part in 10 different Olympic Games.

Millar's first Olympics was in 1972. In 2000, Millar broke his hand. But that didn't stop him. He still competed. He won his first and only medal in 2008. It was silver. His last Olympics was in 2012. He was 65 years old.

Fans called Millar "Captain Canada."

US

Chapter 3

Winter Records

Most speed skaters focus on either short distances or long distances. But Eric Heiden was great at all distances. At the 1980 Winter Olympics, the American won all five speed skating distance events.

Eric Heiden set a record for the 10,000-meter race during the 1980 Olympics.

He became the first person ever to do that.

Gold Standard

Marit Bjørgen is a cross-country skier from Norway. She is the most decorated Winter Olympian ever. In 2018, she won the 15th medal of her career. Eight of Bjørgen's

Fun Fact

Norway has won more medals at the Winter Olympics than any other country. After the 2018 Olympics, Norway had an all-time total of 368.

Marit Bjørgen (1) competed in sprint events and in long-distance events.

medals were gold. She won her last gold medal in the final race of her Olympic career.

Halfpipe Showdowns

Chloe Kim and Shaun White are snowboarding superstars. They hold the highest **halfpipe** scores. In 2018, White scored a 97.75. The highest possible score is 100. He won the gold medal. He's the only

Fun Fact

Eddie Eagan is the only athlete to win a gold medal at both the Summer and Winter Olympics. He won for boxing in 1920, and he won for bobsledding in 1932.

Chloe Kim was the first female snowboarder to land back-to-back 1080s at the Olympics.

person to win three gold medals in halfpipe snowboarding.

Kim beat White's score. She landed a 98.25. That was the highest anyone had ever scored. Kim also won gold. It was her first time at the Olympics.

Rio2016
USA
6
SRBIJA
9
USA
5

Chapter 4

Incredible Careers

No country has had more success at Olympic basketball than the United States. Going into 2020, the US men's and women's teams had won a combined 28 medals.

In 2016, the United States men's basketball team beat Serbia for the gold medal.

From 1996 through 2016, the US women's team won gold at every Summer Olympics.

In 2016, the women's team won its 10th medal. Eight of those medals were gold, one was silver, and one was bronze. The men's team has won even more. Going into 2020, the US men had won 15 gold medals, one silver, and two bronze.

Age Doesn't Matter

Many female gymnasts are in their teens or early 20s. But Oksana Chusovitina proved that age doesn't matter. In 2016, she became the oldest female Olympic gymnast ever. She was 41 years old. Being older than the other gymnasts didn't bother her.

Oksana Chusovitina specializes in the vault.

In 2016, Chusovitina became the first gymnast to compete in seven Olympics. And she was 44 years old when she **qualified** for the 2020 Olympics.

Never Too Old

Oscar Swahn set the record for oldest Olympian. He competed in shooting for Sweden. He was 60 years old when he competed in his first Olympics. At his last Olympics in 1920, he was 72 years old. He won six medals in total.

Fun Fact

In 1896, Greek gymnast Dimitrios Loundras won a bronze medal when he was just 10 years old.

FOCUS ON

Olympic Records

Write your answers on a separate piece of paper.

1. Write a paragraph explaining the main idea of Chapter 1.

2. Which Olympic record do you think is the most impressive? Why?

3. Who won four gold medals for wrestling?

  A. Michael Phelps
  B. Marit Bjørgen
  C. Kaori Icho

4. Why is Eric Heiden's speed skating record so notable?

  A. Most skaters aren't good at short races as well as long races.
  B. Not many people speed skate.
  C. Americans don't win speed skating races.

5. What does **duo** mean in this book?

American volleyball players Misty May-Treanor and Kerri Walsh Jennings were nearly unstoppable. Most experts say they were the best beach volleyball team ever. The ***duo*** *competed in three Olympic Games.*

- A. a large group of athletes
- B. a team of two players
- C. a group of judges

6. What does **decorated** mean in this book?

She is the most ***decorated*** *Winter Olympian ever. In 2018, she won the 15th medal of her career.*

- A. ready for the holidays
- B. award-winning
- C. colorful

Answer key on page 32.

Glossary

archer
A person who competes in archery, using a bow and arrow to shoot at a target.

equestrian
A person who rides a horse.

halfpipe
A U-shaped feature that skiers and snowboarders use to perform tricks by riding up the sides.

individual
For one person, not for a team.

medley
A swimming race that combines all four different strokes. The strokes are butterfly, backstroke, breaststroke, and freestyle.

qualified
Played well enough to take part in a tournament.

wrestler
A person who competes in wrestling. In wrestling, one person tries to pin the other to the ground.

To Learn More

BOOKS

Gitlin, Marty. *Olympic Trivia*. Minneapolis: Abdo Publishing, 2016.

Moon, Derek. *Chloe Kim*. Minneapolis: Abdo Publishing, 2019.

Rule, Heather. *Olympic Games Upsets*. Minneapolis: Lerner Publications, 2020.

NOTE TO EDUCATORS

Visit **www.focusreaders.com** to find lesson plans, activities, links, and other resources related to this title.

Index

Answer Key: 1. Answers will vary; **2.** Answers will vary; **3.** C; **4.** A; **5.** B; **6.** B